I0528711

Travel Like a Pro

Written by
**Mort Greenberg &
Carly Greenberg**

Forward

Welcome to the world of adventure, discovery, and personal growth! As you hold this book in your hands, you hold the key to unlocking travel's endless possibilities. Whether you're a seasoned globetrotter or embarking on your first journey, "Travel Like a Pro" is your companion to discovering the world's wonders with confidence, curiosity, and compassion.

You'll embark on a transformative journey beyond mere sightseeing in these pages. You'll learn how to understand the world through the lens of geography and geopolitics, plan unforgettable itineraries, budget wisely, pack efficiently, and be mindful of cultural differences.

As you navigate the challenges and triumphs of travel, you'll develop valuable skills such as resilience, adaptability, and problem-solving. You'll learn to step out of your comfort zone, embrace uncertainty, and cultivate a sense of wonder and curiosity that will stay with you long after your adventures have ended.

This is a work of fiction. Names, characters, places and incidents either are the product of the author's imagination or are used fictitiously. Any resemblance to actual events or locales or persons, living or dead, is entirely coincidental.

Copyright © 2024 by
Mort Greenberg & Carly Greenberg

Design: Heri Susanto
Illustrations: Dian Kartika Abidin

All rights reserved. No part of this book may be reproduced or used in any manner without written permission of the copyright owner except for the use of quotations in a book review.

First Paperback edition October 2024

Print Paperback ISBN: 978-1-961059-04-7
Kindle KPF ISBN: 978-1-961059-05-4
Ingram EPUB ISBN: 978-1-961059-06-1

Published by TuckEmIn
www.tuckemin.com

Introduction

Tuck Em' In Publishing is a father-and-daughter effort that creates and publishes books for kids. Our mission is to Motivate and Inspire. Our vision is to help kids make the most of their todays and tomorrows.

The Fearless Girl and The Little Guy with Greatness is a book series that aims to share the following message: anything is possible for any kid if they put their mind to it.

Kids, you can find ways to handle yourselves in critical, real-life situations in our books. Caregivers, you will find ways to push the kids in your life to be their best selves. Through our books, we encourage families to communicate more effectively with each other.

"Travel Like a Pro" is the seventh installment in The Fearless Girl and The Little Guy with Greatness book series. This book will move through 14 chapters: 1) Geography and Geopolitics, 2) Crafting a Memorable Travel Experience, 3) Budgeting for Adventures, 4) Packing Light, 5) Dos and Don'ts When Visiting Different Cultures, 6) Language Skills for Travelers, 7) Technology and Travel, 8) Uncovering What Makes a City Unique, 9) Traveling Securely in Any Environment, 10) Avoiding Suspicious People and High Risk Areas, 11) Eating Well and Staying Active, 12) Coping with Homesickness, 13) Making Friends Around the Globe, and 14) Practicing Responsible Tourism and Environmental Stewardship.

Mort Greenberg and his daughter, Carly Greenberg, have embarked on numerous adventures together across the mountains of the United States. They also built self-guided, 18-hour day races in London, Paris, Milan, Venice, Murano, Burano, Rome, Buenos Aires, Tigre, Montevideo, Valparaiso, Santiago, Asuncion, and more.

This father and daughter team has worked through and overcame the same situations that you, as a parent, are experiencing now with a young daughter or son. Each skill in the book is inspired by actual travels over the years from when Carly was eleven to twenty.

You Can Follow Mort and Carly on social media:

@mortgreenberg

@greenbergcarly

@mortgreenberg

@carlygreenberg

This Book Belongs to

_____

Today's Date : _____

Table of Contents

Section 1
Preparing for your Journey

Section 2
Navigating New Destinations

Section 3
Staying Safe and Healthy

Section 4
Connecting with People and Communities

Preparing for Your Journey

Chapter 1

Exploring Your World

An Introduction to Geography and Geopolitics

Welcome, young explorers! Today, we embark on a journey to understand the intricate tapestry of our planet—its lands, people, and the dynamic forces that shape them. In this chapter, we will dive into geography and geopolitics, unraveling the mysteries of our world one layer at a time.

Unveiling Geography

What is Geography?

Geography is more than memorizing maps and capitals; it's about **understanding the Earth and its processes**. It encompasses the study of physical and human landscapes, including natural features like mountains, rivers, and climates, as well as human activities such as population distribution, urbanization, and economic development.

Try it Activities

- Take a blank map and **label** the continents and oceans.

- **Identify and mark** major mountain ranges, rivers, and deserts.

- **Research** and list three unique geographical features of each continent.

The Five Themes of Geography

Geographers use five themes to organize their study of the world: Location, Place, Human-Environment Interaction, Movement, and Region. These themes provide a framework for understanding how various factors interact to shape our planet.

Try it Activities

- Choose a city and describe its location using latitude and longitude **(Location)**.

- Describe the physical and cultural characteristics that make this city unique **(Place)**.

- Discuss how humans interact with the environment in this area **(Human-Environment Interaction)**.

- Investigate the migration patterns of people in this region **(Movement)**.

- Identify any regional patterns or similarities among neighboring countries **(Region)**.

Deciphering Geopolitics

Understanding Geopolitics

Geopolitics **explores the relationship** between geography, power, and politics. It examines how geographical factors influence the behavior of nations, the distribution of resources, and the dynamics of international relations.

Try it Activity

Research a current geopolitical issue and identify the geographical factors involved (e.g., territorial disputes, natural resources) for a place you are about to visit or would like to visit one-day

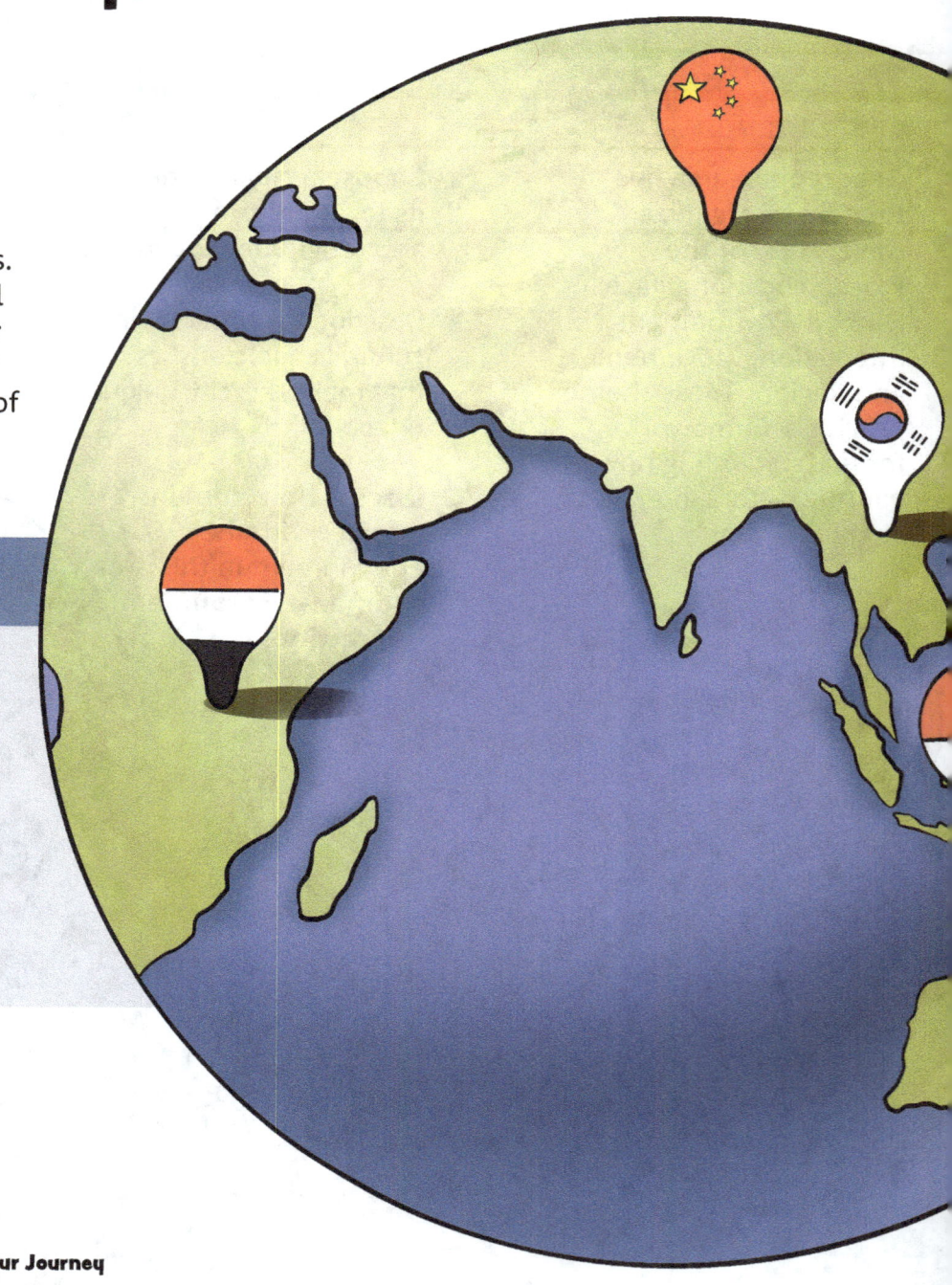

Conclusion

Congratulations! You've taken your first steps into the fascinating worlds of geography and geopolitics. By understanding the Earth's landscapes and the political forces that shape them, you've gained valuable insights into our interconnected world. Keep exploring, keep questioning, and remember that the journey to understanding is endless. Happy exploring, young geographers and geopoliticians!

Chapter 2

Planning Your Itinerary

Crafting a Memorable Travel Experience

Welcome, young adventurers! Today, we embark on a journey to uncover the secrets of crafting the perfect travel itinerary. Whether planning a weekend getaway or a grand expedition, mastering the art of itinerary planning will ensure that every moment of your adventure is filled with excitement and wonder

Setting Your Goals

Defining Your Travel Objectives

Before diving into the nitty-gritty details of your itinerary, **take a moment to clarify your travel objectives**. Are you seeking relaxation, cultural immersion, adventure, or all of the above? To cover more ground each day you may choose to never go inside of some venues. Just walk up, take a picture and then move on to the next site. Understanding your goals will guide your itinerary planning process and help you create a personalized experience.

Try it Activities

- **Write down** three goals you hope to achieve during your trip (e.g., explore historical sites, try local cuisine, connect with nature).

- **Prioritize** your goals in order of importance.

- **Brainstorm** activities and destinations that align with each goal.

Researching Your Destination

Gathering Information

Knowledge is key when planning your itinerary. **Research your destination** thoroughly to uncover hidden gems, must-see attractions, and local customs. Utilize travel guides, websites, and social media to gather insider tips and recommendations.

Try It Activities

- Create a list of attractions and activities you're interested in visiting.

- Research the opening hours, admission fees, and any special events during your travel dates.

- Compile a list of local phrases and customs to enhance your cultural experience.

Mapping Out Your Route

Efficient route planning can save you time and hassle. Plotting your destinations on a map and identifying the most convenient transportation options will ensure smooth transitions between locations.

Try It Activities

- Use an online map to visualize the locations of your chosen attractions.

- Plan your daily itinerary, grouping nearby attractions to minimize travel time.

- Research transportation options (e.g., buses, trains, taxis) and create a daily transportation schedule.

Flexibility and Adaptability

Embracing Spontaneity

While careful planning is essential, leaving room for spontaneity can lead to u**nexpected adventures and memorable experiences**. Be open to serendipitous encounters and be willing to deviate from your itinerary when opportunities arise.

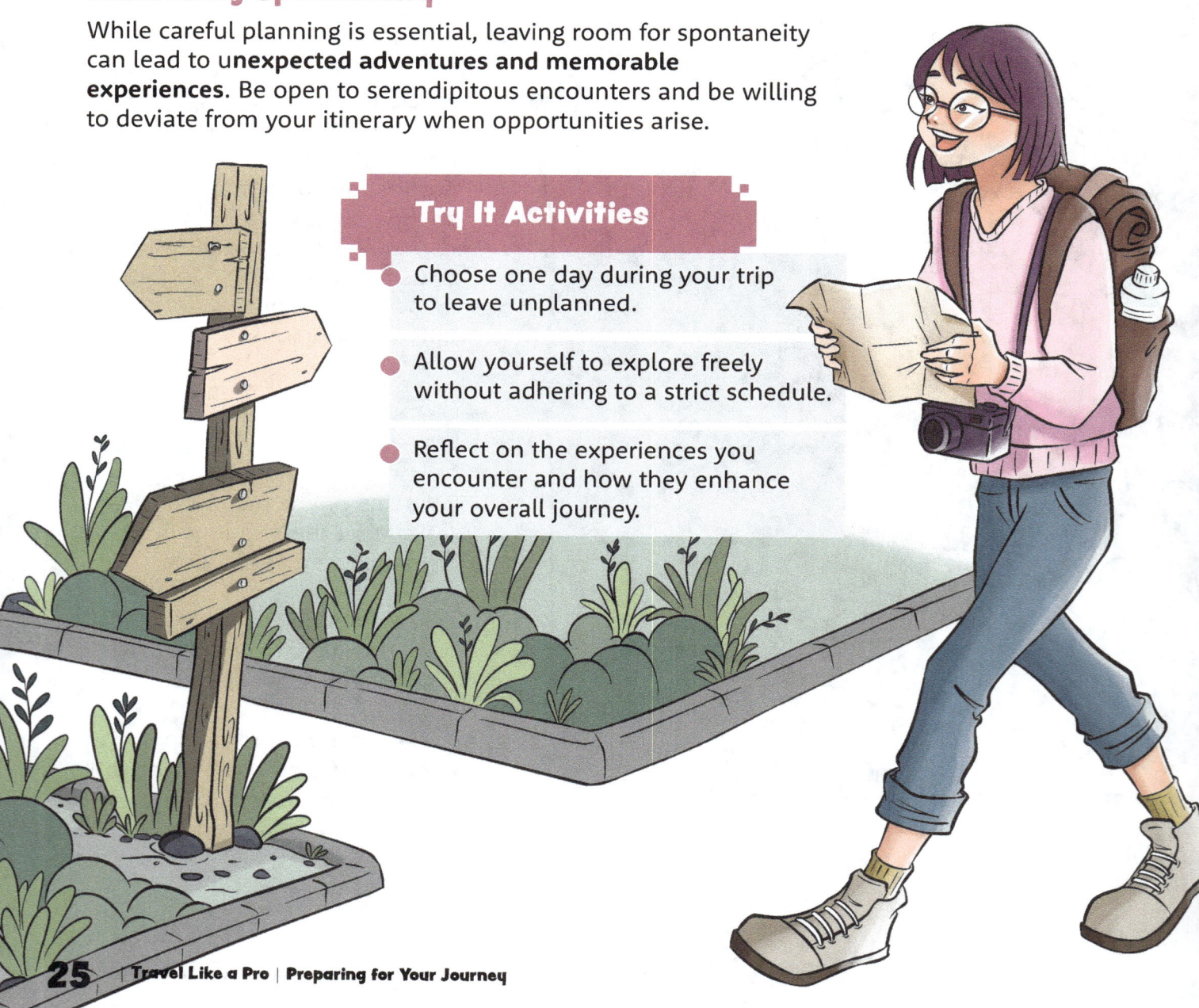

Try It Activities

- Choose one day during your trip to leave unplanned.

- Allow yourself to explore freely without adhering to a strict schedule.

- Reflect on the experiences you encounter and how they enhance your overall journey.

Handling Challenges

Every trip has challenges, whether a missed train or inclement weather. Developing problem-solving skills and maintaining a positive attitude will help you navigate obstacles and turn setbacks into opportunities for growth.

Try It Activities

- Role-play common travel challenges with a friend or family member.

- Brainstorm creative solutions to each scenario, considering resources available in your destination.

- Discuss strategies for staying calm and resilient in the face of adversity.

Building Your Travel Checklist:

Building a travel checklist help create a **smoother and less stress journey**. Having a structured list might just help you prevent last-minute scrambles and avoid forgetting crucial items. Here is our checklist that you can adapt to create your perfect checklist for your trip.

1. Travel Documents

- **Passport** (with at least six months validity)
- **Visas** (if required for your destination)
- **Travel insurance information** (If you need, but not necessary)
- **Itineraries and tickets** (flights, trains, etc.)
- **Hotel booking** confirmations
- **Emergency** contact information
- Copies of all **important documents** (both physical and digital)

2. Health and Safety

- **Vaccination certificates** (check if specific vaccines are required for your destination)
- **Prescription medications** (in original packaging with the prescription)
- Travel health **insurance and documents**
- **First-aid kit** (bandages, antiseptics, etc.)
- **Sunscreen** and insect repellent
- **Hand sanitizer** and masks

3. Finance

- **Foreign currency** of your destination
- **Credit cards** (notify your bank of travel plans and have a # to call if they get stolen)
- **Traveler's checks** (if applicable)
- **Budget plan** for the trip

4. Clothing and Essentials

- **Clothes appropriate** for the climate and culture of the destination
- **Footwear** (comfortable walking shoes, sandals, etc.)
- **Rain gear** (umbrella, raincoat)
- **Swimwear** (if applicable)
- **Sunglasses** and hat

5. Electronics

- Mobile **phone and charger** (Check with your carrier if you will have coverage)
- Power **adapters and converters**
- **Laptop/tablet** and charger (if needed)
- **Camera, memory cards, and charger**
- **Headphones** or earbuds

6. Packing and Luggage

- **Suitcases**/backpack
- Packing **cubes or organizers**
- Luggage **tags and locks**
- **Daypack** for carrying essentials

7. Miscellaneous

- Travel **guidebooks and maps**
- **Snacks**, travel-friendly food and a water bottle
- **Notebooks, Index Cards** (For writing out destinations if there is a language barrier with taxi drivers and others), **notes cards** (A thank you note goes a long way) and pens

8. Just Before You Travel

- **Research and be aware** of any travel advisories
- **Register to inform** your country's embassy or consulate in countries being visited
- Arrange for **care of pets, plants, and home**
- Check **weather conditions** and adjust packing if necessary
- **Confirm** reservations and bookings

Final Challenge:

Plan a mock itinerary for your dream vacation, incorporating the skills and concepts learned in this chapter. Present your itinerary to peers or family members, explaining your rationale behind each decision and soliciting feedback for improvement.

Safe travels, and may your adventures be filled with joy, discovery, and unforgettable moments!"

Conclusion

Congratulations, young travelers! You've unlocked the secrets to crafting a memorable travel experience. By setting clear goals, conducting thorough research, and embracing flexibility, you're ready to embark on adventures that will leave a lasting impression. Bon voyage and happy travels!

Chapter 3

Budgeting for Adventures

Saving and Spending Wisely

Welcome, young explorers! This chapter uncovers the secrets of managing your finances to fuel your adventures without breaking the bank. Whether you're dreaming of a backpacking trip through Europe or a road trip across the country, mastering the art of budgeting will empower you to turn your travel dreams into reality.

Understanding Your Finances

Assessing Your Income and Expenses

Budgeting begins with **understanding your financial situation**. Take stock of your sources of income, whether it's allowance, part-time work, or gifts. Then, track your expenses to determine where your money is going each month.

Try It Activities

- Create a list of your **sources of income**, including any allowances, earnings, or gifts.

- **Track your expenses** for one month, categorizing them into essentials (e.g., food, transportation) and non-essentials (e.g., entertainment, shopping).

- **Calculate** your total income and expenses to determine your monthly savings.

Setting Financial Goals

Identify your short-term and long-term financial goals, including travel aspirations, college savings, or purchasing a big-ticket item. **Having clear objectives** will provide motivation and direction for your budgeting efforts.

Try It Activities

- Write down **three short-term** financial goals (e.g., saving for a weekend getaway, buying a new phone).

- Determine the **cost and timeframe** for achieving each goal.

- Develop a **savings plan**, allocating a portion of your income towards each goal.

Creating A Travel Fund

Establishing a Travel Budget

Once you've defined your travel goals, it's time to create **a dedicated travel budget**. Consider transportation, accommodation, meals, activities, and miscellaneous expenses when estimating travel costs.

Try It Activities

- Choose a destination for your next adventure and research the average transportation, accommodation, and daily expenses costs.

- Calculate the total cost of your trip, including a buffer for unexpected expenses.

- Determine how much you must save each month to reach your travel budget before your departure date.

Building Your Travel Fund

Now that you have a clear target for your travel expenses, **it's time to start saving!** Explore various saving strategies, such as setting up automatic transfers to a dedicated savings account, cutting back on non-essential expenses, and seeking additional sources of income.

Try It Activities

- Open a **separate savings account** specifically for your travel fund.

- Set up **automatic transfers** from your primary account to your travel fund regularly (e.g., weekly or monthly).

- Explore ways to **increase your income,** such as taking on extra chores, selling unused items, or starting a small business.

Smart Spending Strategies

Maximizing Your Savings

Stretch your travel budget further by adopting smart spending habits. Look for **opportunities to save money** on everyday expenses, such as dining out, transportation, and entertainment, without sacrificing quality experiences. If you are able to spend more on a hotel that is a good investment.

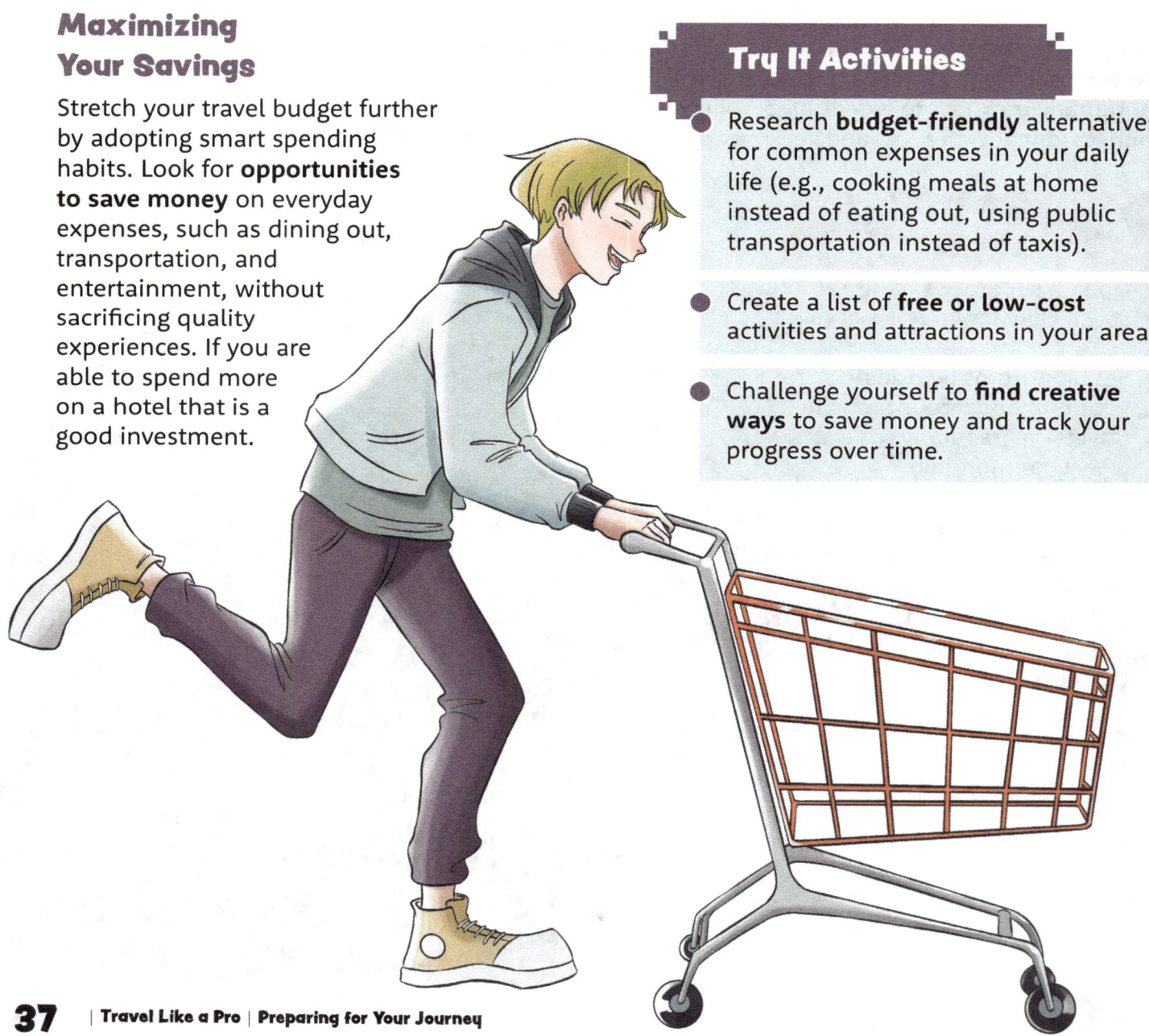

Try It Activities

- Research **budget-friendly** alternatives for common expenses in your daily life (e.g., cooking meals at home instead of eating out, using public transportation instead of taxis).

- Create a list of **free or low-cost** activities and attractions in your area.

- Challenge yourself to **find creative ways** to save money and track your progress over time.

Avoiding Impulse Purchases

Stay mindful of your spending habits and **resist the temptation to make impulse purchase**s that can derail your savings goals. Before making a purchase, ask yourself if it aligns with your priorities and if more cost-effective alternatives are available.

Try It Activities

- Implement a 24-hour **waiting period** for non-essential purchases. If you still want the item after 24 hours, consider whether it's worth the cost.

- Create a list of your **wants versus needs** and prioritize your spending accordingly.

- Practice saying **"no" to unnecessary** expenses and redirecting the money towards your savings goals.

Final Challenge:

Reflect on your current spending habits and identify where to cut back to save money for your next adventure. Implement at least one new saving strategy from this chapter and track your progress over the next month. Share your experiences and insights with a friend or family member and encourage them to join you on your budgeting journey.

Safe travels and happy savings!

Conclusion

Congratulations, young adventurers! By mastering the art of budgeting, you've unlocked the key to turning your travel dreams into reality. With careful planning, smart spending, and discipline, you'll be well-equipped to embark on epic adventures without breaking the bank. Happy travels, and may your journeys be filled with unforgettable experiences!

Chapter 4

Packing Light

Essentials and Tips
for Young Travelers

Welcome, young jet-setters! In this chapter, we'll uncover the secrets to packing like a pro, ensuring that you're prepared for any adventure that comes your way. Whether you're embarking on a weekend getaway or a globetrotting expedition, mastering the art of packing will help you travel easily in style.

Planning Your Packing List

Assessing Your Needs

Before you start packing, take some time to assess your destination, activities, and trip duration. Consider factors such as climate, cultural norms, and planned activities to determine **what items you must bring.**

Try It Activities

- Research the climate and weather conditions of your destination during your travel dates.

- Make a list of essential clothing items based on the forecasted weather.

- Consider any special activities or events you'll participate in and add relevant items to your packing list.

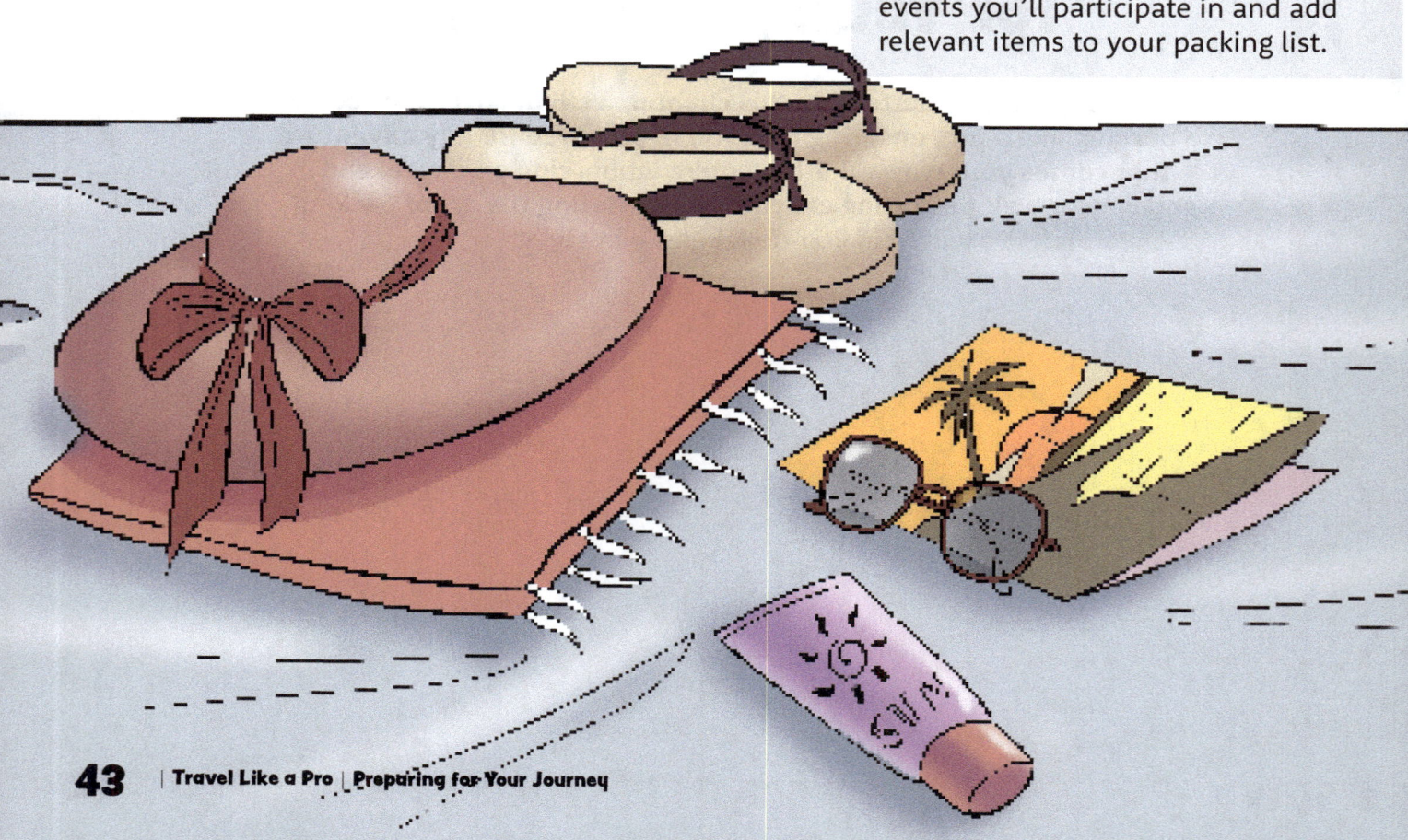

Creating a Packing Checklist

A packing checklist is your best friend for **staying organized** and ensuring you don't forget any essential items. Divide your checklist into categories such as clothing, toiletries, electronics, and documents to cover all your bases.

Try It Activities

- Create a packing checklist template with categories for clothing, toiletries, accessories, electronics, and documents.

- Customize your checklist based on the specific requirements of your upcoming trip.

- Use your checklist to pack for your next adventure, checking off items as you go

Maximizing Space and Efficiency

Choosing the Right Luggage

Selecting the **appropriate luggage** is crucial for a smooth travel experience. Consider factors such as the duration of your trip, mode of transportation, and personal preferences when choosing between a suitcase, backpack, or duffel bag.

Try It Activities

- Assess your upcoming trip and determine the most suitable type of luggage based on your needs.

- Research different luggage options and compare features such as size, weight, durability, and versatility.

- Choose the ideal luggage for your trip and prepare it for packing.

Packing Strategically

Maximize space and minimize wrinkles by employing **smart packing techniques**. Roll your clothes to save space, use packing cubes to organize your belongings, and pack heavier items at the bottom of your bag to distribute weight evenly.

Try It Activities

- Practice rolling your clothes instead of folding them and compare the space-saving benefits.

- Experiment with different packing cube configurations to find the most efficient layout for your luggage.

- Pack your bag using the techniques learned and assess how much space you've saved compared to traditional packing methods.

Essential Items and Travel Tips

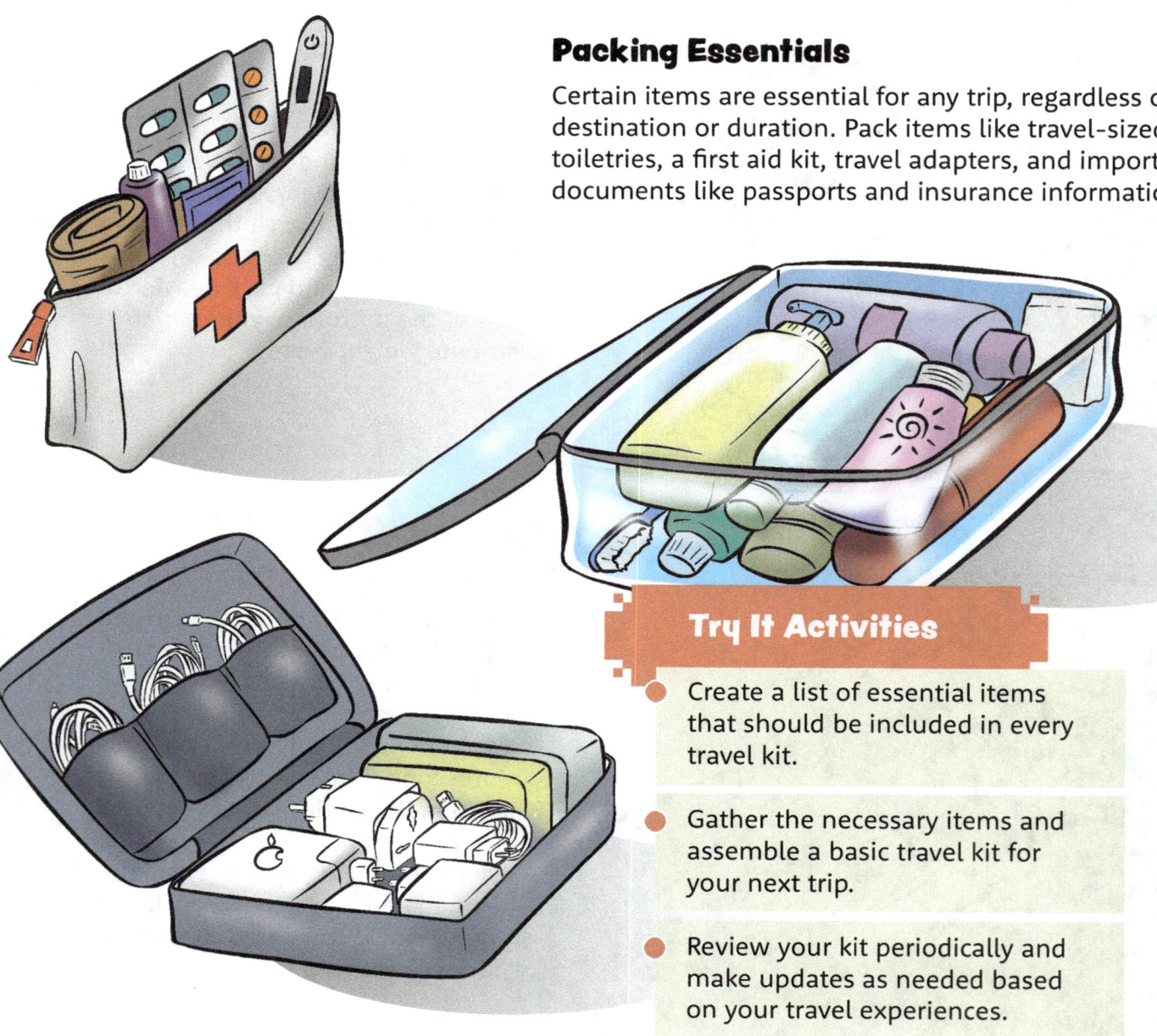

Packing Essentials

Certain items are essential for any trip, regardless of destination or duration. Pack items like travel-sized toiletries, a first aid kit, travel adapters, and important documents like passports and insurance information.

Try It Activities

- Create a list of essential items that should be included in every travel kit.

- Gather the necessary items and assemble a basic travel kit for your next trip.

- Review your kit periodically and make updates as needed based on your travel experiences.

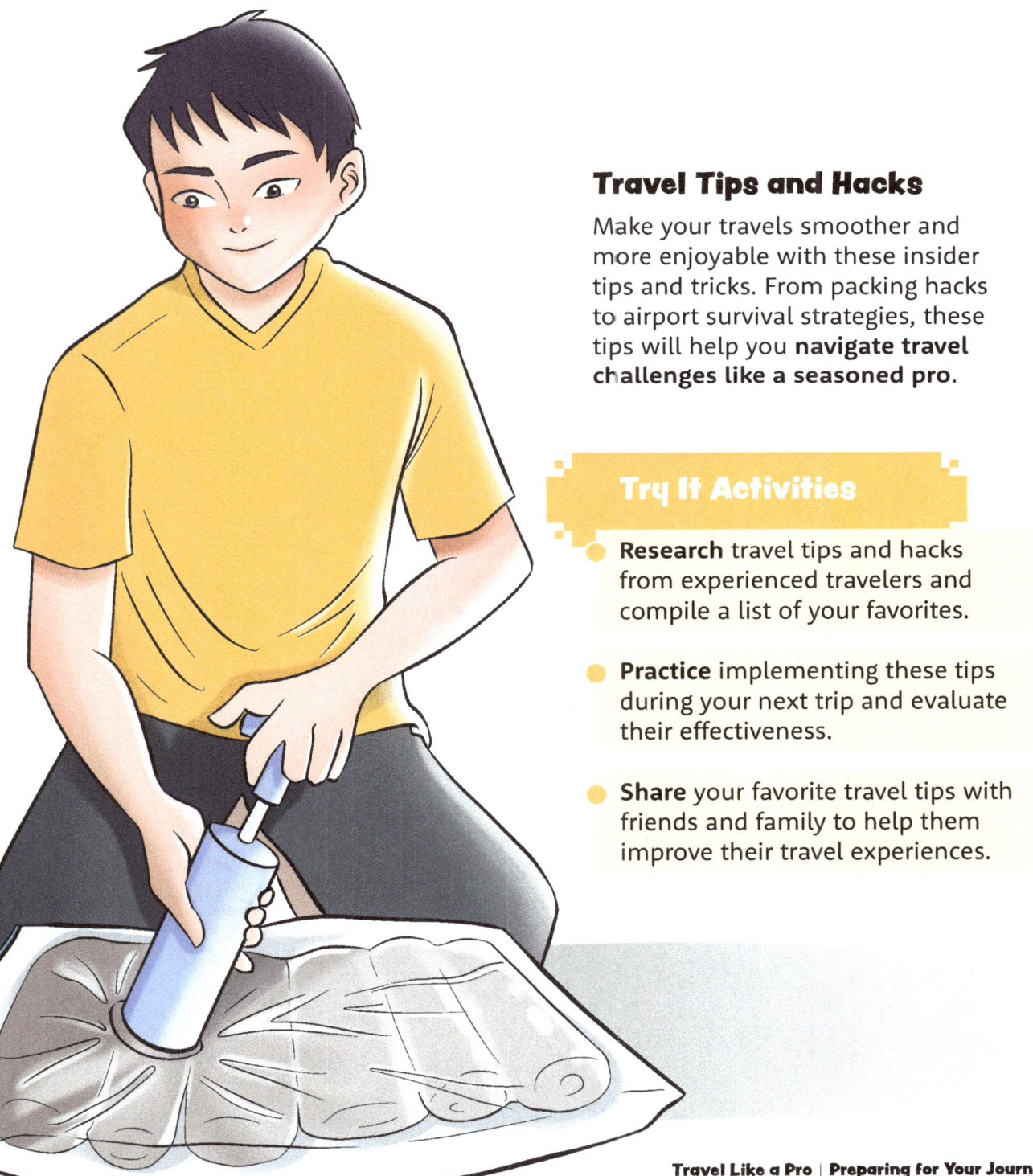

Travel Tips and Hacks

Make your travels smoother and more enjoyable with these insider tips and tricks. From packing hacks to airport survival strategies, these tips will help you **navigate travel challenges like a seasoned pro**.

Try It Activities

- **Research** travel tips and hacks from experienced travelers and compile a list of your favorites.

- **Practice** implementing these tips during your next trip and evaluate their effectiveness.

- **Share** your favorite travel tips with friends and family to help them improve their travel experiences.

Final Challenge:

Plan and pack for a mock trip using the skills and techniques learned in this chapter. Choose a destination, create a packing list, and pack your bag following the strategies outlined. Share your packing success with a friend or family member and offer tips to improve their skills.

Bon voyage and safe travels!

Conclusion

Congratulations, young globetrotters! You've unlocked
the secrets to packing like a pro, ensuring that you're
prepared for any adventure that comes your way. Planning
strategically, maximizing space, and packing essentials will
allow you to embark on epic journeys with confidence and
ease. Happy travels, and may your adventures be filled with
unforgettable moments!

Navigating New Destinations

Chapter 5

Cultural Etiquette 101

Dos and Don'ts When Visiting Different Cultures

Welcome, young travelers, to the world of cultural etiquette! In this chapter, we'll explore the dos and don'ts of interacting respectfully with people from different cultures. Whether exploring a new country or engaging with diverse communities at home, understanding cultural etiquette is essential for fostering meaningful connections and promoting mutual respect.

Understanding Cultural Sensitivity

What is Cultural Etiquette?

Cultural etiquette refers to the **norms, customs, and behaviors considered acceptable and respectful** within a particular culture. It encompasses everything from greetings and gestures to dining customs and social interactions.

Try It Activites

- **Reflect** on a time when you encountered a unfamiliar cultural practice or behavior.

- **Consider** how you reacted and whether your response was respectful and appropriate.

- **Research** the cultural context behind the practice and reflect on what you've learned.

The Importance of Cultural Sensitivity

Cultural sensitivity involves **being aware of and respectful towards cultural differences**, recognizing that what may be acceptable in one culture could be offensive or inappropriate in another. By practicing cultural sensitivity, we can promote cross-cultural understanding and avoid unintentionally offending.

Try It Activities

- **Choose a culture different** from yours and research its customs, traditions, and social norms.

- Reflect on how cultural sensitivity plays a role in **fostering positive interactions and relationships**.

- Brainstorm ways to **demonstrate cultural sensitivity** in everyday interactions with people from diverse backgrounds.

Dos And Don'ts of Cultural Etiquette

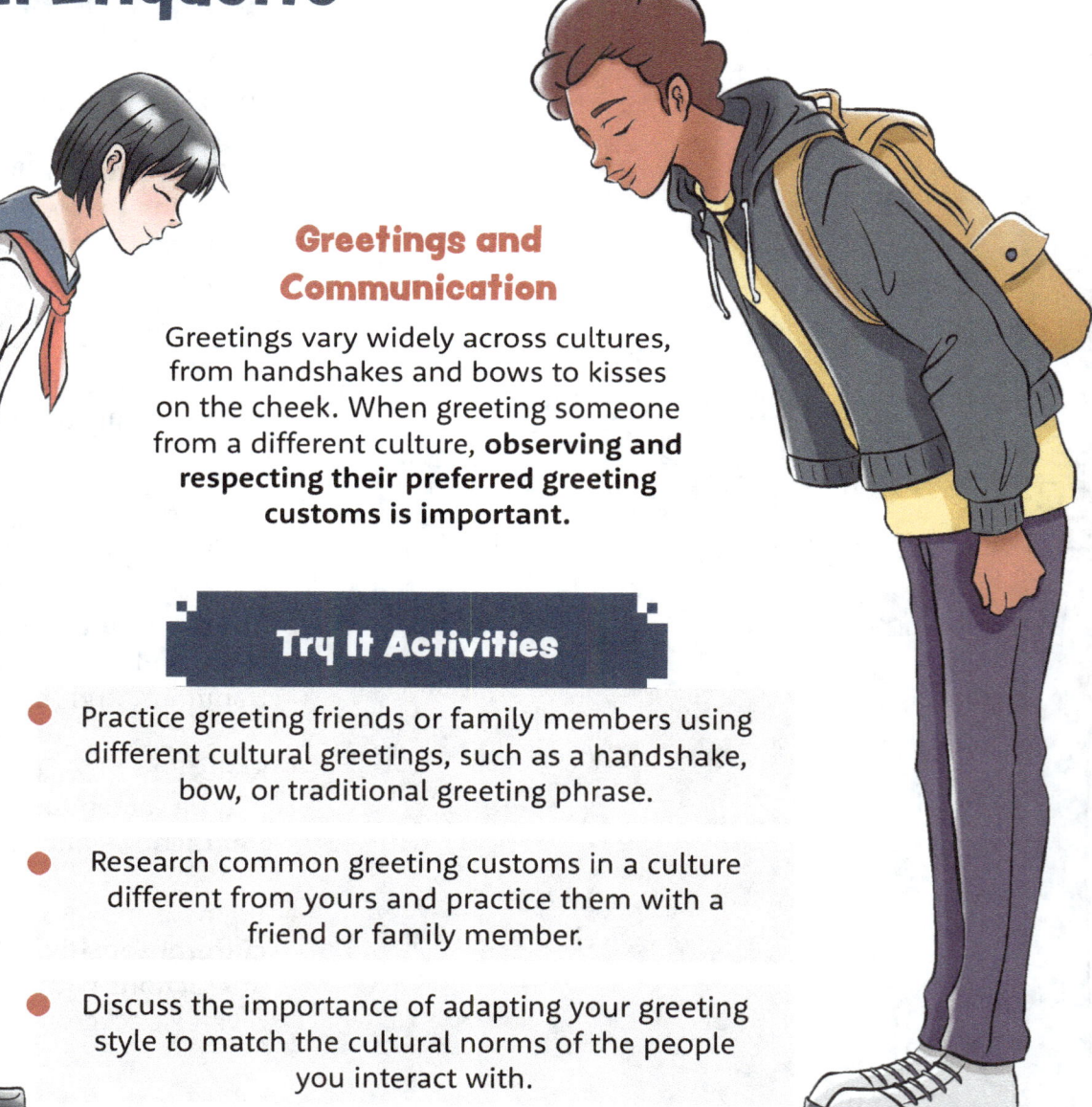

Greetings and Communication

Greetings vary widely across cultures, from handshakes and bows to kisses on the cheek. When greeting someone from a different culture, **observing and respecting their preferred greeting customs is important.**

Try It Activities

- Practice greeting friends or family members using different cultural greetings, such as a handshake, bow, or traditional greeting phrase.

- Research common greeting customs in a culture different from yours and practice them with a friend or family member.

- Discuss the importance of adapting your greeting style to match the cultural norms of the people you interact with.

Dining Etiquette

Dining customs can vary greatly from one culture to another, including table manners, eating utensils, and mealtime rituals. When dining with people from different cultures, observing and following their dining etiquette is essential to **show respect and appreciation for their traditions.**

Try It Activities

- **Research** dining etiquette in a culture different from your own, focusing on table manners, eating utensils, and mealtime customs.

- **Practice** using chopsticks or other traditional utensils commonly used in the culture you're studying.

- **Host** a multicultural dinner with friends or family, incorporating dishes and dining customs from different cultures, and discuss the cultural significance of each.

Embracing Cultural Diversity

Open-mindedness and Respect

Approach interactions with people from different cultures with an open mind and a respectful attitude. **Embrace the opportunity to learn from others** and celebrate the richness of cultural diversity.

Try It Activities

- **Reflect** on a time when you encountered a cultural practice or belief that challenged your perspective.

- **Consider** how you responded to the situation and whether you approached it with an open mind and respect.

- **Identify** ways to cultivate a greater sense of openness and respect towards cultural diversity in your daily life.

Learning from Experience

Cultural etiquette is a lifelong learning process, and each interaction allows us to **expand our understanding and appreciation of different cultures**. Embrace every opportunity to engage with people from diverse backgrounds and learn from their experiences.

Try It Activities

- **Engage** in cultural exchange activities such as language exchange programs, cultural festivals, or community events.

- **Keep** a journal to record your observations, insights, and reflections from these experiences.

- **Share** your experiences with friends or family members and encourage them to join you in exploring and celebrating cultural diversity.

Final Challenge:

Engage in a cultural exchange activity or interaction with someone from a different culture than your own. Reflect on your experience and identify one lesson or insight you gained from the encounter. Share your reflections with a friend or family member and discuss how to apply them to future interactions.

Happy exploring, and may your cultural journeys be filled with growth, understanding, and connection!

Conclusion

Congratulations, young ambassadors of cultural etiquette! By understanding and practicing the dos and don'ts of interacting respectfully with people from different cultures, you're taking an important step towards building bridges of understanding and fostering harmonious relationships in our diverse world. Remember to approach every interaction with curiosity, respect, and an open heart, and you'll be well-equipped to navigate the complexities of cultural diversity with grace and empathy.

Chapter 6

Language Skills for Travelers

Basic Phrases and Communication Tips

Welcome, young globetrotters, to the exciting world of language skills for travelers! In this chapter, we'll explore the importance of basic language proficiency and communication tips that will help you navigate the diverse linguistic landscapes of our world. Whether you're exploring bustling cities or remote villages, mastering key phrases and communication strategies will enhance your travel experiences and foster meaningful connections with people from different cultures.

The Importance of Language Skills

Breaking Down Barriers

Language is a powerful tool that bridges cultural divides and facilitates meaningful interactions. Even a basic understanding of the local language can **open doors and create opportunities for authentic traveling experiences**

Try It Activities

- **Reflect** on a time when language barriers affected your ability to communicate with someone from a different culture.

- **Consider** how learning a few basic phrases in the local language could have improved the interaction.

- **Brainstorm** ways to overcome language barriers and enhance cross-cultural communication in future encounters.

Showing Respect and Appreciation

Learning a few phrases in the local language **demonstrates respect and appreciation for the culture** and customs of the people you encounter during your travels. It shows that you value their language and are trying to connect more deeply.

Try It Activities

- **Research** common greetings and polite phrases in a language spoken in a country you plan to visit.

- **Practice** pronouncing the phrases correctly and memorize their meanings.

- **Reflect** on how learning these phrases can contribute to a more respectful and enriching travel experience.

Basic Phrases for Travelers

Greetings and Introductions

Mastering basic greetings and introductions is **essential for initiating conversations** and building rapport with locals. Learn how to say the following 20+ words / phrases in the language of the places you will be visiting:

"Hello"
"Yes"
"No"
"What is your name?"
"My name is...."
"Nice to meet you"
"Please"
"Thank you"
"I speak a little (name of language)"
"How much does that cost?"

"Where is....?"
"How far"
"I'm sorry"
"Excuse me"
"Can you please repeat that"
"Goodbye"
"I need help"
"Where is the bathroom"
"Where is the train station"

"Do you speak English"
"I am allergic... (Learn words for what you are allergic to)"
- Basic directions: Left, Right, Forward and Backwards
- Know numbers 1 to 10

Try It Activities

- Practice saying **basic greetings and introductions** in the local language, focusing on pronunciation and tone.

- Role-play **common scenarios**, such as meeting someone for the first time or ordering food at a restaurant, using the phrases you've learned.

- Challenge yourself to **initiate conversations** with locals using the phrases you've practiced and observe their reactions.

Asking for Help and Directions

Knowing how to ask for help and directions can be invaluable when **navigating unfamiliar surroundings**. Learn phrases such as *"Excuse me, where is...?"* and *"Can you help me?"* to seek assistance from locals when needed.

ry It Activities

- Role-play asking for **help and directions** in various situations, such as finding a landmark or locating a restroom.

- Practice **active listening** by paying attention to the responses of native speakers and asking follow-up questions if needed.

- Go on a **scavenger hunt** in a familiar area, using the phrases you've learned to ask for directions and navigate to different locations.

Communication Tips for Travelers

Be Patient and Flexible

Navigating language barriers requires patience and flexibility. **Be prepared to encounter misunderstandings** and be willing to adapt your communication style to ensure clarity and understanding.

Try It Activities

- **Reflect** on when you encountered a language barrier while traveling and how you responded to the situation.

- **Consider** how patience and flexibility could have improved the outcome of the interaction.

- **Role-play** challenging communication scenarios with a friend or family member, practicing patience and flexibility in finding solutions.

Use Nonverbal Communication

Nonverbal cues such as **gestures, facial expressions, and body language** can convey meaning and emotion when words fail. Pay attention to cultural norms and use nonverbal communication to enhance your interactions with locals.

Try It Activities

- **Practice** using nonverbal communication cues to convey simple messages, such as indicating "yes" or "no" with a nod or shake.

- **Observe** the nonverbal cues of native speakers during conversations and mimic their gestures and expressions to enhance understanding.

- **Experiment** with using nonverbal communication to express emotions or convey meaning in everyday interactions with friends or family members.

Final Challenge:

Create a language survival guide for a destination you plan to visit, including essential phrases, pronunciation tips, and cultural insights. Share your guide with friends or family and practice using the phrases together. Reflect on how learning basic language skills enhances travel experiences and fosters cross-cultural understanding.

Conclusion

Congratulations, young linguists! By mastering basic language skills and communication tips for travelers, you're well-equipped to navigate the linguistic landscapes of our world with confidence and ease. Remember that every interaction is an opportunity to learn and connect with people from different cultures, so approach each encounter with curiosity, respect, and an open heart. Happy travels, and may your linguistic adventures be filled with enriching experiences and meaningful connections!

Chapter 7

Technology and Travel

GPS, VPNs, and Overall Cybersecurity

Welcome, young adventurers, to the digital age of travel! In this chapter, we'll dive into the essential role of technology in modern-day exploration, focusing on GPS, VPNs, and cybersecurity. From navigating unfamiliar streets to safeguarding your online privacy, mastering technology will enhance travel experiences and keep you safe in an increasingly connected world.

Navigating with GPS

The Power of GPS

Global Positioning System (GPS) technology has revolutionized how we navigate and explore the world. Whether hiking in the mountains or wandering through a bustling city, GPS-enabled devices provide real-time location data and turn-by-turn directions to **help you reach your destination safely and efficiently.**

Try It Activities

- **Familiarize** yourself with the GPS functionality on your smartphone or GPS-enabled device.

- **Practice** using GPS to navigate to a nearby destination, such as a park or cafe.

- **Experiment** with different GPS apps and features to customize your navigation experience.

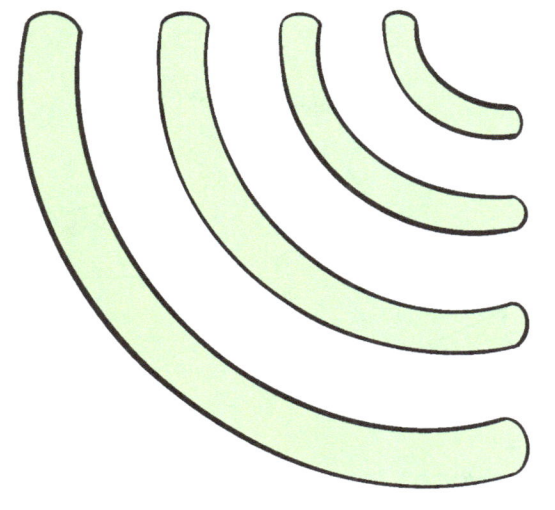

Tips for Using GPS

While GPS technology offers many benefits, it's essential to use it **responsibly and understand its limitations**. Stay aware of battery life, signal strength, and data usage, and always have a backup plan in case of technical issues or emergencies.

Try It Activities

Research common **GPS errors and limitations**, such as signal interference in urban areas or accuracy issues in remote locations.

Create a list of **backup navigation** strategies, such as carrying a physical map or memorizing key landmarks.

Role-play navigation scenarios with a friend or family member, incorporating **GPS and non-GPS techniques** to reach your destination.

Protecting Your Privacy with VPNs

Understanding VPNs

A Virtual Private Network (VPN) encrypts and routes your internet connection through a secure server, **protecting your online privacy and security**. VPNs are particularly useful when traveling, as they prevent hackers and third parties from intercepting sensitive information on public Wi-Fi networks.

Try It Activities

- **Research** how VPNs work and why they're important for protecting your online privacy.

- **Download and install** a reputable VPN app on your smartphone or laptop.

- **Practice** connecting to different Wi-Fi networks while using the VPN and observe how it enhances your online security.

Choosing the Right VPN

Not all VPNs are created equal, so it's essential to research and choose a **reliable provider that meets your needs**. Look for features such as strong encryption, a no-logs policy, and a wide range of server locations for optimal performance.

Try It Activities

- **Research** popular VPN providers and compare their features, pricing, and user reviews.

- Choose a VPN provider that aligns with your **budget and security requirements** and sign up for a subscription.

- Test the VPN on various devices and networks to ensure **compatibility and reliability** before your next trip.

Overall Cybersecurity Tips for Travelers

Securing Your Devices

Protect your smartphones, laptops, and other devices from theft and unauthorized access by implementing strong passwords, enabling device encryption, and using security features such as Find My iPhone or Android

Try It Activities

- Review the **security settings** on your devices and ensure that features such as passcodes, biometric authentication, and encryption are enabled.

- **Practice remotely** locating and locking your device using the Find My iPhone or Android Device Manager feature.

- Develop a habit of regularly **backing up your data** to a secure cloud storage service to prevent data loss in case of theft or damage.

Avoiding Public Wi-Fi Risks

Public Wi-Fi networks are convenient but can pose significant security risks, as hackers may intercept your data over unsecured connections. Whenever possible, use a VPN and avoid accessing sensitive information on public networks.

Try It Activities

- Identify potential risks of using public Wi-Fi networks, such as unencrypted connections and rogue access points.

- Practice connecting to public Wi-Fi networks while using a VPN and observe how it protects your data from potential threats.

- Develop a habit of using cellular data or a personal hotspot when accessing sensitive information in public places.

Final Challenge:

Create a cybersecurity checklist for your next trip, including steps for protecting your devices, using VPNs, and avoiding public Wi-Fi risks. Share your checklist with friends or family members and encourage them to implement these security measures for their travels. Reflect on how practicing cybersecurity enhances your confidence and peace of mind while exploring new destinations.

Safe travels, and may your adventures be filled with excitement, discovery, and digital security!

Conclusion

Congratulations, young tech-savvy travelers! By mastering GPS navigation, using VPNs to protect your online privacy, and implementing cybersecurity best practices, you're well-equipped to explore the world safely and securely. Remember to stay vigilant, practice responsible technology use, and prioritize your safety and privacy while traveling in the digital age.

Chapter 8

Uncovering What Makes a City Unique

Exploring the
Must-See Sites

Welcome, young urban explorers, to the vibrant world of city travel! In this chapter, we'll embark on an exhilarating journey to uncover the must-see sites that make each city unique. From iconic landmarks and historical monuments to hidden gems and local hotspots, exploring a city's must-see sites is an exciting opportunity to immerse yourself in its culture, history, and spirit.

Understanding The Essence of a City

What Makes a City Unique?

Every city has its distinct personality, shaped by its history, culture, geography, and people. Understanding what separates a city is the key to **unlocking its hidden treasures and experiencing its essence.**

Try It Activities

- **Choose a city** you're interested in exploring and research its history, culture, and prominent landmarks.

- Reflect on what **makes the city unique**, such as its architecture, cuisine, arts scene, or natural surroundings.

- Brainstorm a list of **must-see sites** based on your research and personal interests.

Immersing Yourself in Local Culture

Exploring a city's must-see sites isn't just about checking off a list—it's about **immersing yourself in its vibrant culture, connecting with its people**, and experiencing its way of life.

Try It Activities

- Plan a **day of cultural immersion** in your city or a nearby urban area.

- Visit a local museum, art gallery, or historical landmark to learn about the **city's heritage and cultural heritage**.

- Attend **a cultural event, festival, or performance** to experience the city's artistic and creative spirit firsthand.

Exploring Must-See Landmarks

Iconic Landmarks and Monuments

Iconic landmarks and monuments are the heart and soul of a city, **symbolizing its identity and heritage**. From towering skyscrapers and ancient ruins to grand cathedrals and bustling markets, these landmarks capture the essence of a city's history and culture.

Try It Activities

- **Research** the iconic landmarks and monuments of a city you're interested in visiting.

- Create a **scavenger hunt** or sightseeing itinerary that includes visits to these must-see sites.

- Visit each landmark and **document your experiences** through photographs, sketches, or journal entries.

Hidden Gems and Local Hotspots

Beyond the well-known landmarks, every city is filled with **hidden gems and local hotspots waiting to be discovered**. Whether it's a cozy cafe tucked away in a quiet alley, a vibrant street market teeming with life, or a colorful mural adorning a nondescript wall, these hidden treasures offer a glimpse into the soul of a city.

Try It Activities

- **Explore** your city or a nearby urban area with a sense of curiosity and adventure.

- **Wander** off the beaten path and seek out hidden gems and local hotspots recommended by locals or online guides.

- Keep a **travel journal** to document your discoveries and share them with friends or fellow travelers.

Embracing The Adventure of Urban Exploration

Cultivating a Spirit of Adventure

Urban exploration is an adventure like no other, filled with **unexpected discoveries, serendipitous encounters, and memorable experiences**. Embrace the spirit of adventure as you navigate a city's bustling streets, vibrant neighborhoods, and dynamic cultural landscape.

Try It Activities

- Challenge yourself to **explore** a new neighborhood or district in your city each week.

- **Wander and follow your instincts**, allowing yourself to get lost in the maze of streets and alleys.

- Strike up conversations with locals, ask for recommendations, and **be open to serendipitous encounters**.

Practicing Responsible Tourism

As you explore a city's must-see sites, remember to **practice responsible tourism** by respecting local customs, cultures, and communities. Leave no trace, support local businesses, and be mindful of your actions' impact on the environment and residents.

Try It Activities

- **Research** responsible tourism practices and ethical travel guidelines for visiting cities.

- **Create a code of conduct** or checklist for responsible urban exploration, including respecting local cultures, minimizing waste, and supporting sustainable tourism initiatives.

- **Reflect on how** practicing responsible tourism enhances your travel experiences and contributes to the well-being of the cities you visit.

Final Challenge:

Plan an urban exploration adventure in a city you've always wanted to visit or explore a new neighborhood in your city. Create an itinerary that includes visits to must-see sites, hidden gems, and local hotspots, and document your experiences through photographs, sketches, or journal entries. Share your urban exploration adventure with friends or fellow travelers and inspire others to embark on their journeys of discovery and adventure.

Conclusion

Congratulations, young urban adventurers! By uncovering the must-see sites that make each city unique, you're embarking on a journey of discovery, inspiration, and cultural enrichment. Whether exploring iconic landmarks, uncovering hidden gems, or immersing yourself in local culture, urban exploration offers endless opportunities for adventure and growth. So grab your map, lace up your shoes, and embark on an unforgettable journey through the heart and soul of the world's greatest cities!

Embracing Unique Experiences

Chapter 9

Safety First

Tips for Traveling Securely in Any Environment

Welcome, young travelers, to the crucial topic of safety while exploring the world! This chapter will delve into essential tips for traveling securely in any environment. Whether embarking on a solo adventure, exploring with friends, or touring with family, prioritizing safety is paramount to ensure a smooth and enjoyable travel experience. Let's equip ourselves with the knowledge and skills to navigate the world safely and confidently.

Personal Safety Precautions

Stay Aware of Your Surroundings

One of the most effective ways to stay safe while traveling is by **always being aware of your surroundings**. Pay attention to your environment, trust your instincts, and proactively avoid potentially risky situations.

Establish a baseline of what is "normal" for the specific area where you are traveling to. This involves understanding typical traffic patterns, local behaviors, and the general atmosphere. **Be relaxed but be aware of your surroundings to detect anomalies** from the baseline you are expecting.

Utilize **360-Degree Scanning** to check in all directions, not just forward, but also to the your sides and behind. Anything that deviates from the established baseline is considered an anomaly.

This could be an individual behaving erratically, unusual congregations of people, vehicles moving in an atypical pattern, or unattended bags/items.

Try It Activities

- Practice the habit of scanning your surroundings regularly while walking in public spaces.

- Role-play scenarios with a friend where you identify potential hazards or suspicious behavior in a crowded area.

- Reflect on how staying aware of your surroundings can enhance your safety and confidence while traveling.

Trust Your Instincts

Your instincts are a powerful tool for assessing safety and making travel decisions. If something feels off or uncomfortable, **trust your gut and take action** to remove yourself from the situation.

- **Reflect** on when your instincts alerted you to a potentially unsafe situation while traveling or in your daily life.

- **Discuss** with a friend or family member how you responded to your instincts and whether your actions effectively ensured your safety.

- **Role-play scenarios** where you practice listening to and trusting your instincts in various travel situations.

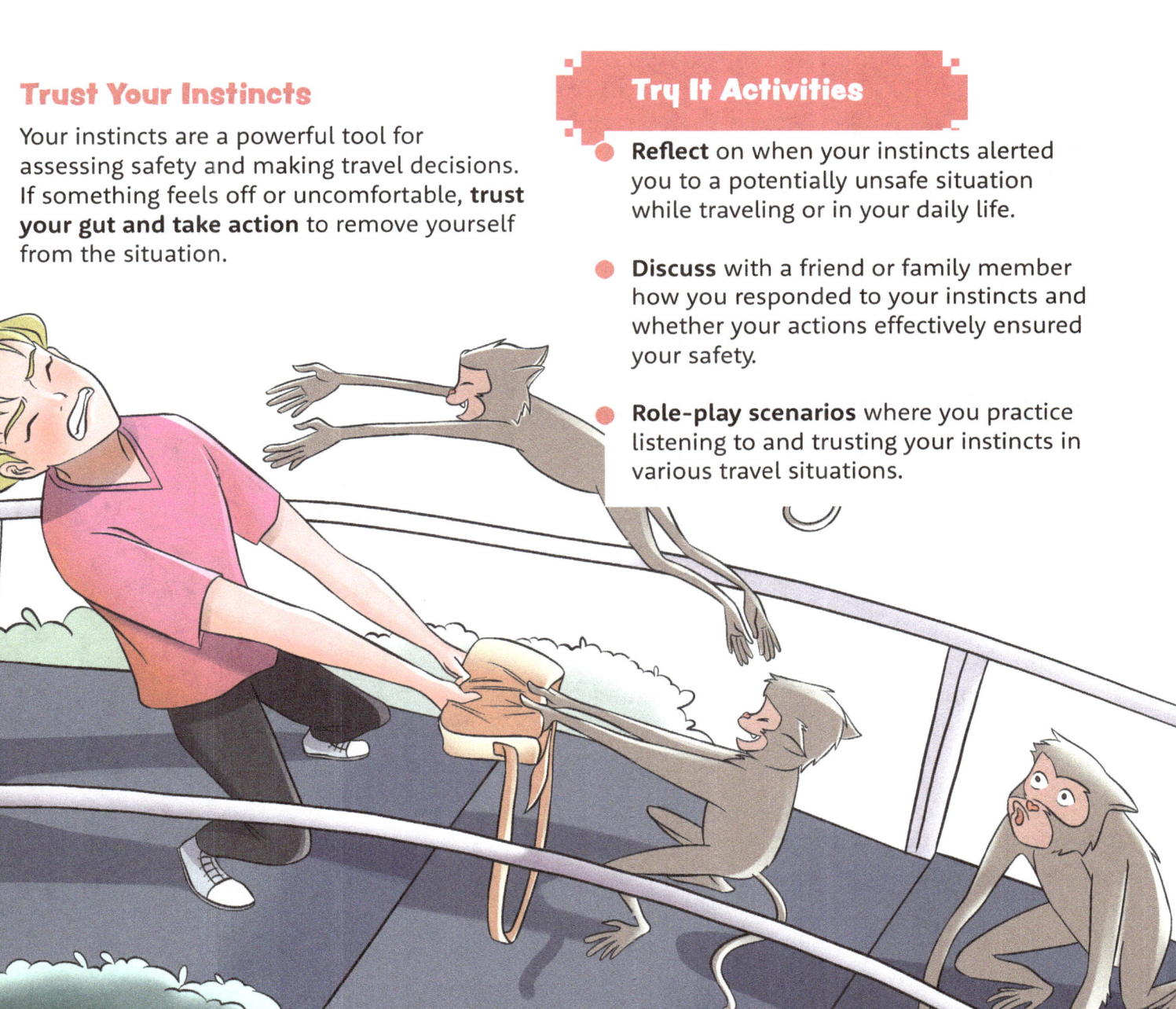

Emergency Preparedness

Have Emergency Contacts and Information Handy

Before embarking on your travels, make sure to have emergency contact numbers, travel insurance information, and local emergency services readily accessible.

Try It Activities

- Create a list of **emergency contacts and information**, including family members, friends, travel insurance providers, and local emergency services for the destinations you plan to visit.

- Store this information in **multiple secure locations**, such as your phone, wallet, and physical notebook.

- **Role-play scenarios** where you practice accessing and using emergency contacts and information in case of an emergency while traveling.

Learn Basic First Aid and Safety Skills

Equip yourself with basic first aid and safety skills to handle minor injuries and emergencies while traveling. Knowledge of CPR, wound care, and basic navigation can be invaluable in times of need.

Try It Activities

- Enroll in a basic first aid and CPR course to learn essential lifesaving skills.

- Practice basic navigation techniques like reading maps and using a compass to find your way in unfamiliar environments.

- Role-play scenarios where you apply first aid and safety skills to respond to common travel emergencies, such as minor injuries or getting lost in an unfamiliar city.

Final Challenge:

Create a personalized safety plan for your next trip, incorporating the tips and exercises from this chapter. Share your plan with a friend or family member and discuss how you can support each other in staying safe while traveling. Reflect on how prioritizing safety enhances your confidence and peace of mind while exploring the world, and commit to making safety a top priority on all your future adventures.

Conclusion

Congratulations, young adventurers, on taking proactive steps to prioritize safety while traveling! You can navigate the world confidently and securely by staying aware of your surroundings, securing your belongings, and being prepared for emergencies. Remember that safety is a priority in any environment, whether you're exploring bustling cities, remote wilderness, or unfamiliar cultures. With the right knowledge, skills, and mindset, you can confidently embark on your travels, knowing that you're prepared to handle whatever comes your way.

Chapter 10

Navigating Safe Travel

Avoiding Suspicious People, Pickpockets, High-Risk Areas, and Activities

Welcome, young travelers, to the crucial topic of navigating safe travel! This chapter will delve into strategies for avoiding suspicious individuals, pickpockets, high-risk areas, and activities while exploring the world. Being proactive and vigilant can protect yourself and ensure a secure and enjoyable travel experience. Let's empower ourselves with the knowledge and skills to navigate the world safely and confidently.

Identifying Suspicious Behavior

Recognizing Warning Signs

Recognizing suspicious behavior is essential for staying safe while traveling. **Trust your instincts and be alert** to signs of potential danger, such as individuals loitering without purpose, excessive attention from strangers, or attempts at distraction or deception.

Try It Activities

- **Study common behaviors** exhibited by pickpockets and scammers, such as creating distractions, invading personal space, or working in groups.

- Role-play scenarios where you **practice identifying suspicious behavior** and responding appropriately, such as moving away from suspicious individuals or seeking assistance from authorities.

- Reflect on how **staying vigilant and trusting your instincts** can help keep you safe in unfamiliar environments.

Seeking Safe Environments

When exploring new destinations, **prioritize safety by seeking out well-lit, populated areas** and avoiding secluded or poorly lit areas, especially at night. Traveling with a trusted companion or group can also enhance safety and provide additional support in unfamiliar environments.

Try It Activities

○ **Research** safety tips and recommendations for the destinations you plan to visit, including information on safe neighborhoods, transportation options, and local safety resources.

○ Practice **planning your routes** and activities to avoid high-risk areas, such as dark alleys, deserted streets, or isolated parks.

○ Role-play scenarios where you practice **navigating safe environments** and making informed decisions about your surroundings while traveling.

Protecting Your Belongings

Securing Your Valuables

Pickpocketing and theft are common risks in tourist destinations, so taking precautions to **protect your belongings is essential**. Keep valuables such as cash, passports, and electronics secure using anti-theft bags, money belts, or hidden pockets.

Try It Activities

- **Experiment** with different methods for securing your valuables, such as using a money belt under your clothing or investing in a slash-resistant bag with locking zippers.

- **Practice** keeping your belongings close and maintaining situational awareness in crowded or high-traffic areas, such as markets, public transportation, or touristattractions.

- Role-play scenarios where you practice **identifying and responding** to potential theft attempts, such as feeling a suspicious hand in your pocket or noticing someone tampering with your bag.

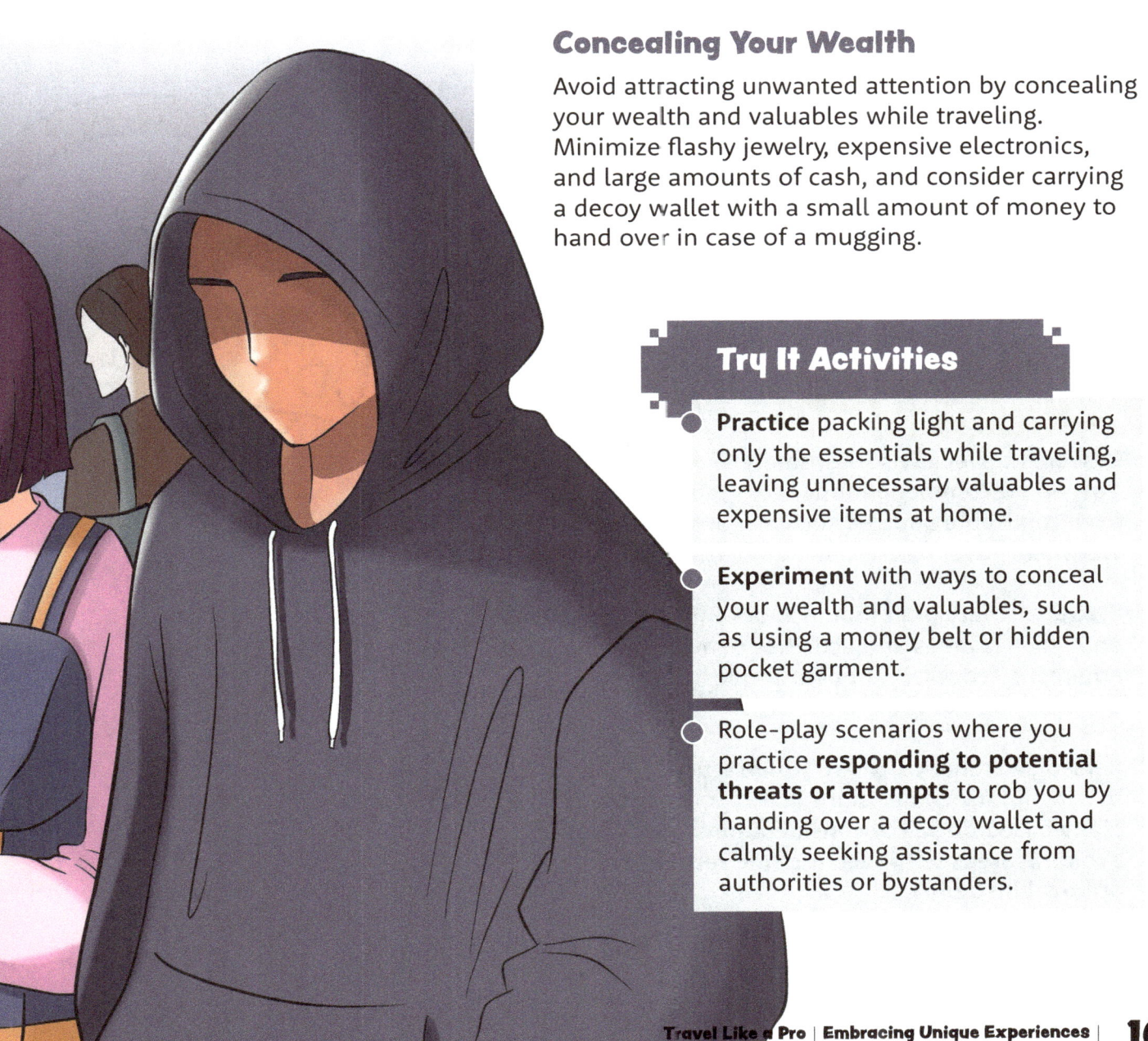

Concealing Your Wealth

Avoid attracting unwanted attention by concealing your wealth and valuables while traveling. Minimize flashy jewelry, expensive electronics, and large amounts of cash, and consider carrying a decoy wallet with a small amount of money to hand over in case of a mugging.

Try It Activities

- **Practice** packing light and carrying only the essentials while traveling, leaving unnecessary valuables and expensive items at home.

- **Experiment** with ways to conceal your wealth and valuables, such as using a money belt or hidden pocket garment.

- Role-play scenarios where you practice **responding to potential threats or attempts** to rob you by handing over a decoy wallet and calmly seeking assistance from authorities or bystanders.

Making Informed Decisions

Researching High-Risk Areas and Activities

Before embarking on your travels, **research potential risks and safety concerns** in the destinations you plan to visit. Stay informed about high-crime areas, political unrest, natural disasters, and other hazards that may affect your safety and well-being.

Try It Activities

- Research travel advisories, safety tips, and recommendations from **reputable sources** such as government websites, travel forums, and guidebooks.

- **Create a safety plan** that includes information on high-risk areas and activities to avoid and emergency contact numbers and resources for the destinations you plan to visit.

- Role-play scenarios where you practice making informed decisions about your travel plans based on safety considerations, such as **avoiding areas with recent crime reports or political instability.**

Trusting Your Intuition

Above all, **trust your intuition and prioritize your safety** and well-being while traveling. If something feels off or uncomfortable, don't hesitate to remove yourself from the situation and seek assistance from trusted authorities or local resources.

Try It Activities

- Practice **tuning into your instincts** and recognizing when something doesn't feel right in a given situation.

- Role-play scenarios where you practice trusting your intuition and **taking proactive steps** to ensure your safety, such as changing your route or seeking assistance from locals or authorities.

- **Reflect** on how trusting your intuition can help keep you safe and empower you to make informed decisions while traveling in unfamiliar environments.

Final Challenge:

Create a safety checklist for your next trip, incorporating the tips and exercises from this chapter. Share your checklist with a friend or family member and discuss how you can support each other in staying safe while traveling. Reflect on how prioritizing safety enhances your confidence and peace of mind while exploring the world, and commit to making safety a top priority on all your future adventures. **Safe travels!**

Conclusion

Congratulations, young adventurers, on taking proactive steps to navigate safe travel and protect yourself from risks and hazards! By being vigilant, informed, and proactive, you can minimize the chances of encountering suspicious individuals, pickpockets, high-risk areas, and activities while exploring the world. Remember that safety is a priority in any environment, whether traveling solo, with friends, or with family. With the right knowledge, skills, and mindset, you can confidently embark on your travels, knowing you have the tools to stay safe and secure wherever your adventures take you.

Chapter 11

Healthy Habits on the Road

Eating Well and Staying Active

Welcome, young adventurers, to the chapter dedicated to maintaining healthy habits while traveling! This chapter will explore the importance of eating well and staying active on the road. Traveling can sometimes disrupt our routines, but by prioritizing our health, we can ensure that our adventures are enjoyable and beneficial for our well-being. Let's dive into strategies for nourishing our bodies and staying active while exploring the world.

Nourishing Your Body with Healthy Eating

Making Smart Food Choices

Eating well while traveling is essential for **maintaining energy levels, supporting immune function, and feeling your best**. Make smart food choices by choosing nutritious, balanced meals that provide essential vitamins, minerals, and macronutrients.

Try It Activities

- Research healthy eating options and **local cuisine** in the destinations you plan to visit.

- Create a **list of nutritious foods and ingredients** to look for while dining out or shopping for groceries.

- Practice **reading food labels and menus** to identify healthier options and make informed choices about what to eat.

Staying Hydrated

Hydration is key to maintaining energy, supporting digestion, and preventing dehydration while traveling. Carry a **reusable water bottle and aim to drink plenty of water** throughout the day, especially in hot or humid climates or during physical activities.

Try It Activities

- **Calculate** your daily hydration needs based on age, weight, activity level, and climate.

- Practice staying hydrated by carrying a reusable water bottle and **setting reminders** to drink water regularly throughout the day.

- Experiment with **different ways to infuse water** with flavor, such as adding fresh fruit, herbs, or cucumber slices, to make hydration more enjoyable and refreshing.

Incorporating Fruits and Vegetables

Fruits and vegetables are rich in essential nutrients and antioxidants that support overall health and well-being. Aim to incorporate **a variety of colorful fruits and vegetables** into your meals and snacks while traveling to ensure you're getting a wide range of vitamins and minerals.

Try It Activities

- Experiment with **different ways to incorporate fruits and vegetables** into your meals and snacks, such as adding them to salads, smoothies, or sandwiches.

- Create a list of **locally available fruits and vegetables** in the destinations you plan to visit and make a point to try new varieties and flavors.

- Role-play scenarios where you **practice ordering or preparing meals** that include a variety of fruits and vegetables to ensure you're getting adequate nutrition while traveling.

Staying Active and Fit On The Road

Finding Opportunities for Physical Activity

Staying active while traveling doesn't have to mean hitting the gym. Look for **opportunities to incorporate physical activity** into your daily routine, such as walking, hiking, biking, or exploring outdoor attractions.

Try It Activities

- **Research outdoor activities** and recreational opportunities in the destinations you plan to visit, such as hiking trails, bike paths, or parks.

- **Create a list** of physical activities you enjoy and would like to try while traveling, such as swimming, yoga, or dancing.

- **Role-play scenarios** where you incorporate physical activity into your daily itinerary, such as scheduling a morning jog or exploring a city on foot instead of using public transportation.

Practicing Mindful Movement

Mindful movement practices such as yoga, tai chi, or stretching can help **improve flexibility, reduce stress, and promote relaxation while traveling**. Incorporate brief stretching or mindfulness exercises into your daily routine to stay grounded and centered on the road.

Try It Activities

- Experiment with different **mindful movement practices**, such as yoga poses, tai chi movements, or deep breathing exercises.

- Create a **short daily routine** of mindful movement exercises to practice while traveling, incorporating stretches, poses, or breathing techniques that help you feel grounded and relaxed.

- Role-play scenarios where you integrate mindful movement practices into your daily routine, such as starting each day with a brief yoga session or taking breaks for stretching and deep breathing while exploring new destinations.

Prioritizing Rest and Recovery

Getting Adequate Sleep

Quality sleep is essential for overall health and well-being, especially while traveling. Prioritize rest and aim to get adequate sleep each night to support physical and mental recovery, optimize cognitive function, and ensure you have the energy to enjoy your adventures to the fullest.

Try It Activities

- Create a **bedtime routine** to help you wind down and prepare for sleep while traveling, incorporating activities such as reading, journaling, or listening to calming music.

- Experiment with different strategies for **improving sleep quality**, such as adjusting your sleep environment, limiting screen time before bed, or practicing relaxation techniques.

- Role-play scenarios where you prioritize rest and practice your bedtime routine while traveling, ensuring you get the sleep you need to **feel refreshed and rejuvenated daily**.

Managing Stress and Practicing Self-Care

Traveling can be exciting and stressful. **Practice self-care and stress management techniques** to help you stay calm, centered, and resilient in the face of challenges or unexpected obstacles while on the road.

- Create a **self-care toolkit** with activities and strategies that help you manage stress and promote relaxation, such as meditation, journaling, or spending time in nature.

- Practice incorporating **self-care activities** into your daily routine while traveling, taking breaks to rest, recharge, and reconnect with yourself.

- Role-play scenarios where you encounter stressful situations or challenges while traveling and practice using self-care **techniques to stay calm and grounded** in the moment.

Final Challenge:

Create a personalized plan for maintaining healthy habits while traveling, incorporating the tips and exercises from this chapter and ***book #5, Wellness Warriors in the Fearless Girl and the Little Guy with Greatness series***. Share your plan with a friend or family member and discuss how you can support each other in staying healthy and active while exploring the world. Reflect on how prioritizing your health enhances your travel experience and commit to making healthy choices on all your future adventures.

Safe travels, and stay healthy!

Conclusion

Congratulations, young adventurers, on prioritizing your health and well-being while traveling! By nourishing your body with healthy eating, staying active and fit, and prioritizing rest and recovery, you're setting yourself up for a fulfilling and enjoyable travel experience. Remember that maintaining healthy habits on the road is important for your physical health and overall happiness and well-being. With the right mindset, knowledge, and dedication, you can continue to explore the world with energy, vitality, and joy.

Chapter 12

Coping with Homesickness

Strategies for Overcoming Feelings of Discomfort

Welcome, young travelers, to the chapter dedicated to understanding and managing homesickness while exploring the world! In this chapter, we'll explore the common experience of feeling homesick while away from home and share strategies for overcoming these feelings of discomfort. Homesickness is a natural part of travel, but with the right mindset and coping techniques, you can navigate these emotions and enjoy your adventures to the fullest. Let's dive in and discover how to cope with homesickness effectively.

Understanding Homesickness

Recognizing Homesickness

Homesickness is a common **emotional response to being away from home and familiar surroundings**. It can manifest as loneliness, sadness, longing, or nostalgia for the comforts of home, family, and routine.

Try It Activities

- Reflect on a **time when you experienced homesickness**, whether while traveling, attending summer camp, or being away from home for an extended period.

- Identify the **specific emotions and sensations** you felt during that experience, such as sadness, longing, or a desire for familiarity.

- **Journal about your reflections** and how you coped with homesickness during that time, noting any strategies or techniques that helped alleviate your discomfort.

Normalizing Homesickness

Homesickness is a **normal and natural response to being away from home**, especially during periods of transition or adjustment. Understanding that many people experience homesickness can help normalize your feelings and reduce feelings of isolation or shame.

Try It Activities

- Research the **prevalence of homesickness and common triggers** for these feelings among travelers, students, and individuals living away from home.

- Discuss your findings with friends or family members and **share personal experiences of homesickness** to normalize the experience and support one another.

- Reflect on how **understanding the universality of homesickness** can help you feel less alone and more resilient in coping with these emotions while traveling.

Coping Strategies For Homesickness

Stay Connected with Loved Ones

Connecting with family and friends back home can provide comfort and support while traveling. **Make an effort to stay in touch** through phone calls, video chats, or messaging apps to share updates and stay connected to your support network.

Try It Activities

- **Schedule regular check-ins** with family and friends back home to stay connected and share updates about your travels.

- Experiment with **different methods of communication**, such as video calls, voice messages, or handwritten letters, to stay connected in meaningful ways.

- **Role-play scenarios** where you reach out to loved ones for support during moments of homesickness, sharing your feelings, and seeking encouragement and reassurance.

Create a Sense of Home Away from Home

Bringing familiar comforts and routines with you while traveling can help create a sense of home away from home. **Pack meaningful items** such as photos, a favorite book, or a comforting blanket to remind you of home and provide comfort during moments of homesickness.

Try It Activities

- Create a **travel kit of comforting items and mementos from home**, such as photos, a favorite stuffed animal, or a journal filled with memories.

- **Designate a space in your accommodation** for personalizing and making it feel more like home, such as setting up a bedside table with familiar items or hanging up photos and decorations.

- Role-play scenarios where you **engage in self-soothing activities or rituals** that remind you of home, such as listening to familiar music, reading a favorite book, or practicing a relaxation technique.

Embracing The Adventure of Travel

Focus on the Present Moment

Practice mindfulness and **focus on the present moment** to fully immerse yourself in your travel experiences and distract yourself from feelings of homesickness. Engage your senses, appreciate your surroundings, and savor travel's unique experiences and opportunities.

Try It Activities

- Practice **mindfulness techniques** such as deep breathing, body scans, or mindful walking to anchor yourself in the present moment and reduce feelings of homesickness.

- **Create a travel journal** or scrapbook to document your experiences, thoughts, and emotions while traveling, focusing on the positive moments and memorable experiences.

- **Role-play scenarios where you practice** being present and fully engaged in your travel experiences, letting go of worries about home, and embracing the adventure of the moment.

Seek Out New Connections and Experiences

Embrace the opportunity to meet new people, explore new places, and try new activities while traveling. **Building connections with fellow travelers, locals, or expats** can provide a sense of community and belonging that helps combat feelings of homesickness.

Try It Activities

- **Engage in social activities** and group tours to meet fellow travelers and locals with similar interests and passions.

- **Volunteer or participate** in cultural exchange programs to connect with local communities and immerse yourself in new experiences and perspectives.

- Role-play scenarios where you **initiate conversations and make new connections** with people you meet while traveling, sharing stories, experiences, and insights to foster meaningful connections and combat feelings of homesickness.

Final Challenge:

Create a personalized homesickness coping plan for your next trip, incorporating the tips and exercises from this chapter. Share your plan with a friend or family member and discuss how you can support each other in managing homesickness while traveling. Reflect on how practicing coping strategies enhances your resilience and well-being while exploring the world, and commit to implementing these.

Conclusion

Congratulations, young adventurers, on exploring strategies for coping with homesickness and navigating travel's emotional ups and downs! By understanding the nature of homesickness, normalizing your feelings, and practicing coping strategies, you can effectively manage homesickness and continue to enjoy your adventures with confidence and resilience. Remember that homesickness is a natural part of the travel experience, and it's sometimes okay to feel sad or lonely. With patience, self-compassion, and support from loved ones, you can overcome homesickness and embrace the joys and challenges of exploring the world.

Connecting With People and Communities

Chapter 13

Making Friends Around the Globe

Building Relationships
with Fellow Travelers

Welcome, young adventurers, to the chapter dedicated to the art of making friends while traveling! In this chapter, we'll explore the joys of connecting with fellow travelers worldwide and share strategies for building meaningful relationships on the road. Making friends while traveling can enrich your experiences, broaden your perspective, and create lasting memories. Let's dive in and discover how to forge connections with fellow adventurers wherever your travels take you.

Embracing The Spirit of Adventure

Embracing Openness and Curiosity

Approach each travel experience with an **open mind and a spirit of curiosity**, ready to engage with people from diverse backgrounds and cultures. Be open to new experiences, perspectives, and friendships that may enrich your journey.

Try It Activities

- Reflect on times when you felt hesitant or shy about approaching new people while traveling. **Identify any fears or insecurities** that may have prevented you from making connections.

- Practice **stepping out of your comfort zone** by initiating conversations with fellow travelers or locals during your next trip.

- Role-play scenarios where you **practice approaching strangers and striking up conversations**, focusing on being genuine, curious, and open to learning about their experiences and perspectives.

Embracing Shared Experiences

Shared experiences are a powerful catalyst for **building connections with fellow travelers**. Whether exploring a new city, embarking on an adventure activity, or sharing a meal, bonding over shared experiences can foster camaraderie and friendship.

Try It Activities

- Seek opportunities to **participate in group activities**, tours, or excursions where you can connect with fellow travelers with similar interests and passions.

- Reflect on **memorable experiences** you've shared with friends or family while traveling and consider how these shared moments strengthened your relationships.

- Role-play scenarios where you **engage in group activities** or shared experiences with fellow travelers, focusing on building rapport, sharing stories, and creating meaningful connections.

Building Rapport and Connection

Practicing Active Listening

Listening attentively and showing genuine interest in others is key to **building rapport and connection with fellow travelers**. Practice active listening by focusing on the speaker, asking questions, and empathizing with their experiences.

Try It Activities

- Practice active listening skills by **engaging in conversations with friends**, family, or classmates and focusing on listening without interrupting or formulating responses.

- Role-play scenarios where you practice active listening with fellow travelers, **asking open-ended questions** and showing genuine interest in their stories and experiences.

- Reflect on how practicing active listening enhances your **ability to connect with others** and build meaningful relationships while traveling.

Finding Common Ground

Finding common ground with fellow travelers can help **bridge cultural and linguistic barriers** and create a foundation for building rapport and connection. Look for shared interests, experiences, or values you can bond over.

Try It Activities

● Reflect on your interests, hobbies, and passions, and **identify common themes or topics** you enjoy discussing.

● Practice finding common ground with fellow travelers by initiating conversations about **shared interests or experiences**, such as favorite travel destinations, hobbies, or cultural experiences.

● Role-play scenarios where you **connect with fellow travelers over shared interests**, engaging in conversations and activities that bring you closer together.

Nurturing Relationships and Staying Connected

Exchanging Contact Information

Exchange contact information with fellow travelers to stay in touch and continue **building relationships beyond your travels**. Social media, messaging apps, or email are convenient ways to stay connected with friends from around the globe.

Try It Activities

- Practice **exchanging contact information** with fellow travelers you meet during your adventures, using social media platforms or messaging apps to stay connected.

- Reflect on the **importance of maintaining relationships** with fellow travelers and how staying connected can enrich travel experiences and foster long-lasting friendships.

- Role-play scenarios where you exchange contact information with fellow travelers, expressing your desire to **stay in touch and continue building your friendship** beyond your travels.

Planning Reunions and Future Adventures

Stay connected with fellow travelers by **planning reunions or future adventures**. Whether meeting up in a new destination or embarking on a group trip, planning future adventures can keep your friendships alive and thriving.

Try It Activities

- **Discuss potential reunion** or travel plans with fellow travelers you've connected with during your adventures, exploring possibilities for future meetups or joint travel experiences.

- Create a **shared travel bucket list** with friends from around the globe, highlighting destinations and experiences you'd like to explore together.

- **Role-play scenarios** where you plan reunions or future adventures with fellow travelers, discussing logistics, itineraries, and shared goals for your travels together.

Final Challenge:

Create a plan for making friends and building connections with fellow travelers during your next trip, incorporating the tips and exercises from this chapter. Share your plan with a friend or family member and discuss how you can support each other in making meaningful connections while traveling. Reflect on how building friendships enhances your travel experiences and commit to fostering new relationships on all your future adventures.

Safe travels and happy friendships!

Conclusion

Congratulations, young adventurers, on exploring the art of making friends while traveling and discovering the joys of connecting with fellow travelers from around the globe! By embracing openness and curiosity, practicing active listening, and nurturing relationships with fellow adventurers, you can build meaningful connections that enrich your travel experiences and create lasting memories. Remember that friendships can blossom in the most unexpected places, so keep an open heart and a welcoming spirit as you embark on your adventures worldwide.

Chapter 14

Leaving a Positive Impact

Practicing Responsible Tourism and Environmental Stewardship

Welcome, young explorers, to the chapter dedicated to understanding the importance of responsible tourism and environmental stewardship while traveling! In this chapter, we'll delve into the concept of positively impacting the places we visit and the environment we explore. By practicing responsible tourism, we can minimize our ecological footprint, support local communities, and contribute to the preservation of natural and cultural heritage. Let's embark on a journey to learn how to make a difference while exploring the world.

Understanding Responsible Tourism

Defining Responsible Tourism

Responsible tourism involves traveling in a way that **minimizes negative impacts on the environment**, respects local cultures and communities, and maximizes the benefits to both travelers and host destinations. It encompasses ethical considerations, sustainable practices, and a commitment to leaving a positive legacy for future generations.

Try It Activities

- Reflect on your past travel experiences and consider how your actions may have **impacted the places you visited** and the people you encountered.

- Research the **principles of responsible tourism** and identify key concepts such as sustainability, ethical tourism, and community engagement.

- Role-play scenarios where you practice making responsible choices while traveling, such as **supporting local businesses, minimizing waste, and respecting cultural norms and traditions.**

Recognizing the Importance of Environmental Stewardship

Environmental stewardship involves taking responsibility for protecting and preserving natural resources and ecosystems. By practicing environmental stewardship, travelers can help **conserve biodiversity, reduce pollution, and mitigate the impacts of climate change** on fragile ecosystems.

Try It Activities

- Research **environmental issues and challenges** facing the destinations you plan to visit, such as deforestation, marine pollution, or habitat destruction.

- Reflect on the **interconnectedness of environmental issues** and how individual actions can contribute to positive or negative outcomes for ecosystems and wildlife.

- Role-play scenarios where you **practice environmental stewardship** while traveling, such as participating in beach cleanups, reducing plastic waste, or supporting conservation initiatives.

Practicing Responsible Tourism

Supporting Local Communities

One of the most significant ways travelers can positively impact is by supporting local communities and economies. By purchasing goods and services from local businesses, engaging in cultural experiences, and respecting local customs and traditions, travelers can **contribute to host communities' economic empowerment and cultural preservation**.

Try It Activities

- **Research local businesses and community-led initiatives** in the destinations you plan to visit, such as artisan cooperatives, ecotourism projects, or social enterprises.

- Create a budget for your trip that includes **allocations for supporting local businesses** and community-based tourism initiatives.

- Role-play scenarios where you **interact with local vendors, artisans, and tour guides**, practicing respectful and responsible tourism behaviors such as bargaining ethically, seeking permission before taking photos, and engaging in cultural exchanges.

Minimizing Ecological Footprint

Reducing our ecological footprint is essential for preserving natural ecosystems and minimizing environmental impact. By adopting sustainable travel practices such as **reducing waste, conserving energy and water, and choosing eco-friendly transportation options**, travelers can help mitigate the negative effects of tourism on the environment.

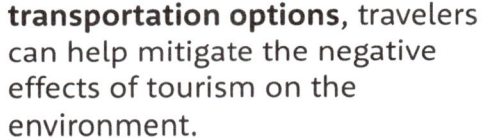

Try It Activities

- Create a **sustainable travel packing list** that includes reusable items such as water bottles, cloth bags, and eco-friendly toiletries.

- Practice **minimizing waste** while traveling by opting for reusable products, avoiding single-use plastics, and disposing of waste responsibly.

- Role-play scenarios where you practice **sustainable transportation** options such as walking, biking, or using public transportation, and reflect on how these choices contribute to reducing your ecological footprint.

Leaving a Lasting Legacy

Educating and Inspiring Others

As responsible travelers, we can educate and inspire **others to make positive choices and advocate for sustainable tourism practices**. By sharing our experiences, knowledge, and passion for responsible travel, we can empower others to become stewards of the environment and champions for positive change.

Try It Activities

- Reflect on your travel experiences and **identify key lessons** learned about responsible tourism and environmental stewardship.

- Create a **social media campaign** or blog post sharing your insights and experiences with responsible travel, using photos, videos, and storytelling to engage and inspire others.

- Role-play scenarios where you **converse with friends, family, or classmates about responsible tourism** and environmental stewardship, sharing your experiences and encouraging them to make a positive impact while traveling.

Supporting Conservation and Preservation Efforts

Supporting conservation and preservation efforts is vital for protecting natural and cultural heritage sites for future generations. By volunteering, donating, or participating in conservation projects, travelers can **contribute to the preservation of biodiversity, cultural heritage, and natural landscapes.**

Try It Activities

- **Research conservation organizations** and initiatives in the destinations you plan to visit, such as wildlife reserves, national parks, or historical landmarks.

- **Create a fundraising or volunteer plan** to support conservation efforts during your travels, whether through donations, volunteer work, or participation in conservation projects.

- Role-play scenarios where you **engage in conservation activities** such as tree planting, wildlife monitoring, or habitat restoration, and reflect on the importance of supporting these efforts to preserve natural and cultural heritage.

Final Challenge:

Create a responsible tourism action plan for your next trip, incorporating the tips and exercises from this chapter. Share your plan with a friend or family member and discuss how you can support each other in practicing responsible tourism and environmental stewardship while traveling. Reflect on how your actions positively impact the places you visit and the environment you explore and commit to making responsible choices on all your future adventures.

Safe travels and happy stewardship!

Conclusion

Congratulations, young stewards of the earth, on exploring the principles of responsible tourism and environmental stewardship! By practicing responsible tourism, supporting local communities, minimizing your ecological footprint, and leaving a lasting legacy of conservation and preservation, you can make a positive impact while exploring the world. Remember that small actions can lead to significant change, and each choice you make as a traveler has the power to shape the future of our planet. Let's commit to leaving a positive legacy for future generations and preserving the beauty and diversity of our world for all to enjoy.

In Closing...

As we come to the final pages of "Travel Like a Pro," it's time to reflect on the journey we've embarked upon together. Throughout this book, we've covered geography, navigated the intricacies of cultural etiquette, and honed the skills needed to embark on unforgettable adventures. But beyond the practicalities of travel, we've also explored the profound impact that exploration can have on our lives and the world around us.

Travel is more than just a series of destinations on a map; it's a journey of self-discovery, personal growth, and connection. It's about stepping out of our comfort zones, embracing the unknown, and opening ourselves up to the world's endless possibilities. Along the way, we've learned valuable lessons about resilience, adaptability, embracing diversity and cultural understanding.

Think about the power of travel to unite us as global citizens, transcending borders, languages, and cultures. In a world often divided by differences, travel uniquely reminds us of our shared humanity and interconnectedness. It teaches us that no matter where we come from or where we're headed, we are all part of the same journey, bound together by our love for exploration and discovery.

Wherever your travels may take you, may you always find joy, inspiration, and a sense of home in our world's vast and beautiful tapestry. Ready, set, roam!

About The Authors

For the past 25 years **Mort Greenberg** has been a salesperson and sales manager for technology start-ups and larger media companies. Fighting his way up from an Account Executive to a role as a division President you can guess there were many challenges that needed to be overcome. Along the way Mort launched two companies, FitAd and MindFlight and learned many hard-fought lessons that start-ups are not always successful. He is a graduate of the State University of New York at New Paltz where he studied International Relations and Economics. While in college he started a company selling screen printing and promotional items to local businesses and on-campus organizations. At the same time, he also volunteered as a Congressional District Intern for the U.S. House of Representatives. He is an Eagle Scout and in junior high school bought several newspaper routes from neighborhood kids to create his first business. Mort is also the author of Revenue Vs. Sales, a three book series that you can find on Amazon.com.

Carly Greenberg attends the University of Maryland's Smith School of Business with a double major in marketing and management. Carly's twin brother has autism, and she has helped him find his voice through her unique interactions with him. He is the original little guy with greatness. Carly is the original fearless girl, always helping others, volunteering, and finding ways to do more with less - all while having to put up with a crazy dad. Carly also holds a black belt in Tae Kwon Do.

www.ingramcontent.com/pod-product-compliance
Lightning Source LLC
Chambersburg PA
CBHW081002140626
46546CB00018B/2946